AF131344

BOOK ANALYSIS

Written by Sabrina Zoubir
Translated by Rebecca Neal

The Girl On Paper

by Guillaume Musso

GUILLAUME MUSSO

FRENCH AUTHOR

- **Born in Antibes in 1974.**
- **Notable works:**
  - *Lost and Found* (2007), novel
  - *The Girl on Paper* (2011), novel
  - *7 Years Later* (2012), novel

Guillaume Musso was born in Antibes in the south of France in 1974, and knew from a very early age that he wanted to be a writer. A trip to New York when he was 19 proved a formative experience, providing him with many ideas for his novels. He studied economics at university, and taught the subject until 2008. His breakout novel, *Afterwards...* (2004), has sold over a million copies and been translated into over 20 languages to date. His subsequent novels, including *A Mix-Up in Heaven* (2005), *Will You Be There?* (2006) and *Lost and Found* (2007), also proved a hit with readers and cemented his position as one of France's most popular contemporary novelists. A number of his books have been adapted for the cinema.

THE GIRL ON PAPER

A COMPELLING BLEND OF FANTASY AND REALITY

- **Genre:** novel
- **Reference edition:** Musso, G. (2012) *The Girl on Paper*. Trans. Aitken, A. and Boyce, E. London: Gallic Books.
- **1ˢᵗ edition:** 2010
- **Themes:** writing, separation, friendship, love, depression, the supernatural

The Girl on Paper was published in the spring of 2010 to popular and critical acclaim, with many reviewers considering it one of Musso's best novels to date. It combines fantasy and reality to tell the story of Tom Boyd, a writer who is going through a difficult patch in his life and feeling adrift. This all changes when Billie Donnelly, the heroine of one of his novels, falls through the page and suddenly materialises in his living room. Thanks to this surprising encounter, Tom gradually rediscovers his zest for life and love of writing.

SUMMARY

A MAN WHO HAS LOST HIS WAY

Tom Boyd is the author of the bestselling Angel Trilogy, but despite his professional success, his life is falling apart: Aurore, the woman he loves, has left him; he is suffering from writer's block as his devoted readers and his editor eagerly await the third instalment in the series; and his drug use, drinking and arrest make perfect tabloid fodder. Fortunately, he can still count on his loyal friends Carole and Milo, who grew up with him in the tough MacArthur Park neighbourhood of Los Angeles. However, their well-meaning advice and attempts to help him seem to fall on deaf ears. Milo is especially worried because he has to break some important news to Tom: they have already spent the sizeable advance he received for the third book, and the money that Milo tried to invest "went up in smoke with the Madoff affair" (p. 47). Tom is stunned by his friend's revelation and quickly comprehends the gravity of the situation: if he finishes his book the sales will easily pay off the advance, but if he does not overcome his writer's block, the empire he and Milo spent years building will collapse, leaving them both mired in debt. However, he is still reeling from his breakup with Aurora and feels powerless to do anything. He is so desperate that he tries to commit suicide by overdosing on pills.

This first part of the story also reveals a detail that will turn out to be crucial later on: Milo tells Tom that the printer set off the print run of the special edition of his last book too early, meaning that there are 100 000 defective copies in circulation, with a story that stops "abruptly on page 266, midway through a sentence" (p. 43).

TOM MEETS BILLIE

Tom, who thought that he had ended it all, is woken up by a nightmare in the middle of the night. A storm is raging outside and the wind has blown the living room window open. He closes the window to stop water from getting in and goes into the kitchen, where he quickly realises that he is not alone. He is astonished to see a woman who looks exactly like Billie Donnelly, the heroine of his novel, and who tells him that she has fallen from the pages of his book. He then bombards her with questions to make sure that she really is who she says she is (he writes detailed biographies of all his characters and stores them on his computer, where only he can access them). She passes the test with flying colours, but Tom is still hesitant to believe that she is real, because by the time Carole and Milo come over she has left his apartment, leaving no sign that she was ever there. His two friends think that he is exhausted from overwork and encourage him to see his psychiatrist.

We later find out that the whole thing is a ruse devised by Milo to save his friend: he gave a struggling aspiring actress named Lilly Austin $15 000 to enter Tom's life in the role of Billie.

Later on, Billie manages to convince Tom that she is real and persuades him to go to Mexico to find Aurore, who is currently on holiday there.

A PACT AND A BLOSSOMING FRIENDSHIP

Tom accepts Billie's plan and sets out for Mexico. However, first of all they strike a tacit pact: Billie tells Tom that she will help him to find Aurore and win her back if he will change the plot of his story to suit her. She wants to leave behind the unfulfilling life he has set out for her by moving from the oncology department into paediatrics and having Jack, the man she is in love with, leave his wife to move in with her. He agrees, and the ups and downs of their trip to Mexico bring them closer, creating a real bond between them. Meanwhile, Carole and Milo grow worried about Tom and set out to look for him.

While Tom, Carole, Milo and Billie are in the hotel's clifftop restaurant, they realise that Aurore is staying in the same hotel with her new boyfriend, the Formula 1 champion Rafael Barros. Later on, Tom gets the chance to talk things over with her while Carole and Milo talk about their own feelings. However, at this stage of the story neither of these relationships fundamentally change.

Rafael proposes to Aurore in the middle of the restaurant, but she turns him down. Tom looks on from a distance and is happy with the outcome, until Rafael lashes out in humiliation and punches him in the face.

Billie seems to be coming down with something, and her symptoms are worrying: she is tired, has a fever and keeps shivering, and eventually vomits ink.

BILLIE'S ILLNESS

The printing company has sent out the order to have all the defective copies of the Angel Trilogy destroyed. Milo, Tom and Carole come to realise that this decision is somehow linked to Billie's illness, and that the only way to save her is to get their hands on the copy of the book that the printer sent to Tom, which is the only one that has not been destroyed yet. However, Tom threw the book out and it was found by a woman who then sold it online. The friends embark on a round-the-world chase to get hold of the book, which is being passed from reader to reader. Tom then realises that the story needs to continue if he wants to save Billie. This gives him fresh inspiration, and he starts writing again. He also realises that he has fallen in love with his character. He eventually finishes the novel and Billie makes a full recovery.

Billie leaves reality to go back to the fictional

world, Tom's new book is a hit, and Carole and Milo get married. It seems that order has been restored. However, Milo cannot shake his feeling of guilt and confesses the truth about Billie (who is really Lilly Austin) to Tom, who is dumbfounded by this revelation. Although he is initially furious with his friend, he finally decides to set out to look for Lilly, and goes to Boston, where she is studying. However, when he sees her looking happy with another man, he leaves without speaking to her. Instead, he decides to tell her story in a novel, which he calls *The Girl on Paper*. Lilly reads the novel and, as she reciprocates Tom's feelings, she decides to find him at a book signing. They are finally reunited and leave together.

CHARACTER STUDY

TOM BOYD

Tom Boyd, the novel's main character, is a successful author who is suffering from writer's block and dealing with a difficult breakup. After he became a bestselling author, he began a relationship with Aurore Valancourt, a famous pianist with a turbulent love life who soon leaves him for another man. This pushes Tom over the edge, and the reader soon sees that he is a depressed, extremely fragile man who struggles to face up to his inner demons. In spite of his success, he lacks self-confidence and is still scarred by his difficult past: "Despite how far we had come from those days, a part of me was still that fifteen year-old from MacArthur Park, with its dealers, its dropouts and its stairwells filled with shouting and screaming" (p. 33).

Although he has his problems, Tom is a sincere, loyal and devoted friend who will go to any lengths to support the people he cares about. As we find out in the novel, he has even killed to protect his best friend. He is passionate and throws himself wholeheartedly into his romantic relationships (even though his breakup with Aurore plunges him into depression, at the end of the novel he gets on the first plane to Boston so that he can see Billie, his new love interest). He is somewhat introverted, and does not much care for the trappings of fame (he also delegates the management of his career to Milo). Although he is going through a difficult period at the beginning of the novel, his life revolves around writing.

CAROLE ALVAREZ

In spite of her difficult past, Carole has managed to make something of her life. As a child she was repeatedly raped by her stepfather, who was murdered when she was 15, and she spent her teenage years in a run-down, dangerous neighbourhood. Nonetheless, she still tried to find a way out and demonstrated extraordinary strength of character in doing so. As well as studying hard, she constantly moved between different living arrangements and took on a string of odd jobs. She was a brilliant student and "passed her exams to get into the police academy the first time round, joining the LAPD on her twenty-second birthday" (p. 53), before "climbing the ladder incredibly quickly" (*ibid.*). By the time the story unfolds, she is a detective for the LAPD. She is very close to Milo and Tom, whom she considers her only family, and has shared a painful secret with Tom for several years (nobody else knows that her stepfather abused her or that Tom was responsible for keeping her alive by inventing the magical universe of the Angel Trilogy for her). She eventually tells Milo to assuage the jealousy he feels at her and Tom's secret, and ends up marrying and starting a family with him.

MILO LOMBARDO

Although the three friends shared the same sense of purposelessness when they were growing up, Milo undoubtedly had the most violent childhood. His mother is Irish and his father is Mexican, and at the age of 12 he joined the MS13, "an extremely violent gang" whose initiation ritual is "a hazing that for girls was a gang rape and for boys a group beating that lasted around fifteen minutes" (p. 55). During his time in the gang, he stole cars, sold drugs, extorted local businesses and trafficked weapons. However, he finally breaks free of his old life thanks to "Tom's intelligence and Carole's tenderness" (p. 56). He owes his success chiefly to his own intelligence, as he becomes Tom's agent when he is starting out as a writer and teaches himself the basics of the job. His friend's career as a bestselling novelist is due in large part to his drive, determination and talent.

Tom says: "In the competitive world of publishing he had learned his trade on the job, with no experience and no qualifications to help him, and had become one of the best" (p. 41). Like Carole and Tom, Milo is completely devoted to the people he cares about, and is exceptionally ambitious on Tom's behalf, "believing in me more than I believed in myself" (*ibid.*).

ANALYSIS

FICTION AS ESCAPISM

The novel depicts fiction as an essential alternative to a bleak reality. It is vital because it is more than a way of forgetting the tedium of everyday life: for each of the novel's characters, fiction quite literally becomes their lifeline. Specifically, Tom's success as a writer lifts the three friends out of poverty and their difficult lives in the impoverished, violent neighbourhood they grew up in, the story Tom writes for Carole gives her the strength to go on living, and Billie's appearance pulls Tom back from the brink of suicide. We could go even further and say that the story also saved Billie's life, since we find out from Milo that the invented story allowed the doctors to find out that she was actually suffering from a serious heart defect and save her life.

It is therefore understandable that Tom would decide to write this surprising story down in a novel so that his readers can also benefit from fiction's capacity to heal.

That said, in one key passage, Billie complains to Tom that fiction is too boring compared to reality: "In real life, everything has more taste, more substance to it. [...] Everything in fiction is so bland. [...] You might be very good at telling stories, creating emotions, pain, heartache, but you don't know how to describe the spice of life, its flavours" (p. 159).

This makes us question the escapism and fantasy worlds that fiction can provide, and ask ourselves whether they can really compare to real life.

WRITING AND THE ROLE OF THE WRITER

The difficulty of writing

The novel's depiction of the writer's profession is far from idealised, as it presents an author who was previously riding high as a bestselling novelist, but now finds himself at a loss for inspiration and unable to write. In doing so, Musso demonstrates the unpredictability of an art form that can never be truly mastered, or rather that is intrinsically linked to a host of external criteria that often lie outside the writer's control. In this case, a relatively mundane event (a breakup) is enough to leave the author unable to write and drive him to observe: "But reality was still there: I was still being eaten alive by my grief and I hadn't written anything in over a year. My mind felt blocked, paralysed into inactivity. Words no longer came to me, any will to write had deserted me, my imagination had dried up" (p. 38). He later explains that: "I had never needed chemical stimulation to write [...]. When I was on a roll, nothing else mattered: I was in a different place, in a trance, in a kind of hypnotic dream. During these fertile periods, writing itself became a drug, more euphoric than the purest coke, more delightful than the most intoxicating drunkenness. But all of that felt very far away now. I had given up writing and writing seemed to have given up on me" (pp. 148-149).

The novel presents writers' relationship to their craft as inherently conflict-ridden, and writing is often described in terms more appropriate to human relationships: "any will to write had deserted me", "writing seemed to have given up on me", and so on. It is as though writing is a person who is locked in combat with the writer.

Write or die

In the novel, writing is more than just work or a passion: it consumes the writer's entire life. Tom tries to explain this to Milo with a somewhat clumsy comparison: "Writing a book isn't like building a car or making washing powder" (p. 50). However, Milo keeps insisting that he needs to rediscover his will to write, because for him this is the same thing as his will to live: "And, anyway, writing is your life. It's your best hope for getting out of your depression!" (p. 46).

For months, nothing can shake Tom out of his torpor and get him to write again; he only finds fresh inspiration when he realises that he is in love with Billie and that she will die if he does not finish his book. As he explains to Milo, Billie is "fading away in an environment that's foreign to her", and the only way to save her is to "send her back to the fictional world by writing the third volume of the trilogy of the book. That's her 'doorway out' of the real world" (p. 250). In other words, not writing will lead to death. Musso places significant emphasis on this symbolic representation of what writing means to the writer. Having said that, love is the real driving force behind Tom's progress: "I could see now that my feelings for Billie had lifted the curse. By giving me a foothold back in the real world, she'd found the key to unlock my mind" (p. 275).

An ode to friendship

Although literature and writing are the story's main themes, friendship is the glue holding it together. The opening lines of the novel's first chapter demonstrate Milo's concern for his best friend: when he knocks on Tom's door, as he has done every night for the past several months, and is once again met with silence, he decides to act. However, this raises a moral conundrum: as he breaks into the house, he wonders "Do you have the right to save your friends from themselves?" (p. 27). This question is at the heart of the story. Milo chooses to answer in the affirmative, and considers nothing off limits as he attempts to save his friend: "apart from Carole, Milo had only ever had one friend and he was prepared to do anything to help him forget his heartache and start living again" (pp. 27-28).

The idea behind "the girl on paper", and therefore behind the novel, comes from Milo's commitment to his friend. Milo, Carole and Tom became friends when they were children living in Los Angeles's impoverished MacArthur Park neighbourhood. They are all aware that, without their bond, they would probably have gone astray and certainly would not have experienced such exceptional social mobility, and this feeling comes through in many of their conversations. For example, Milo tells Tom: "You've always been the sensible one. [...] You've stopped me from making more than one mistake in the past. If it weren't for you, I would have ended up in prison, or worse, ages ago. If it weren't for you, Carole would never have become a cop. And if it weren't for you, I would never have been able to buy my mother a house" (p. 33).

However, this is not how Tom sees things: "Milo was the backbone of our little business. [...] He always said that he owed everything to me, but I knew that it was really the other way round: he was the one who had made me into a star by getting my first book onto all the bestseller lists" (p. 41). This comment is telling: the two friends seem to depend on one another, and it appears that one person's success is only made possible by the other's friendship. Their bond with Carole is just as strong, and at the end of the story we learn that Tom even shot her abusive stepfather in the head.

This ode to friendship is most clearly expressed in the speech Tom delivers at his two best friends' wedding in the novel's closing pages:

> "Milo, we've been through everything together, from the tough times growing up, right up until we 'made it to the top' and all that jazz. [...] Over the last year, the two of you have shown me that I can always count on you, no matter what. You've shown me that the old saying about friendship doubling joy and halving grief is more than just a neat phrase." (p. 363)

A MIX OF GENRES

In the few years since his first novel was published, Guillaume Musso has become one of France's bestselling authors. His novels enjoy print runs of several hundred thousand copies and have been translated into some 30 languages. One of the reasons for his success is his style, which blends several contemporary literary genres, with fantasy and suspense predominating. This has allowed him to win over many readers, who are transported into a world where anything seems possible.

Readers have also responded enthusiastically to the dynamism of Musso's writing. He seeks to constantly keep his readers on the edge of their seats and guide them seamlessly through to the story's conclusion. To do this, he opts for simple, direct vocabulary and sentence structures, short chapters and very visual descriptions, so that readers almost feel as though they are watching a film.

FURTHER REFLECTION

SOME QUESTIONS TO THINK ABOUT...

- According to Tom Boyd, what is the reader's role and responsibility?
- The novel's main character is a writer who falls in love with his heroine. What do you make of this? What does this tell us about literature?
- How is the theme of travel treated in the novel?
- Why can *The Girl on Paper* be described as a popular novel? Support your answer using specific examples.
- The novel contains the following quote, from the film director Tim Burton: "People ask me when I'm going to make a film with real people. What's real?" (p. 105). Basing your answer on the story of *The Girl on Paper*, how would you respond to this question?
- Social climbing is another of the novel's underlying themes. What message(s) does Musso aim to transmit to his readers through the

example of Tom, Milo and Carole?

- At the end of the novel, Tom finds out that Billie is not actually the heroine of his novel, but a real person. However, they still fall in love. What conclusion can we draw from this?
- When Billie asks Tom to change the plot of his novel, he says: "So now I found myself in a mess of my own making. You can't suddenly give a character in a book a completely different personality. I may have been the author, but that didn't make me God. Fiction goes by its own rules [...]" (p. 293). Comment on this quotation.
- What would you say that the novel is a metaphor for?

We want to hear from you!
Leave a comment on your online library
and share your favourite books on social media!

FURTHER READING

REFERENCE EDITION

- Musso, G. (2012) *The Girl on Paper*. Trans. Aitken, A. and Boyce, E. London: Gallic Books.

www.brightsummaries.com

Ebook EAN: 9782808007627

Paperback EAN: 9782808007962

Legal Deposit: D/2018/12603/22

Cover: © Primento

Digital conception by Primento, the digital partner of publishers.